The Wealth Game

6 Foundational Principles for Mastering the Game of Wealth

Thomas M. Ransome

The Wealth Game

Thomas M. Ransome

ISBN: 979-8-87844447-7 (Paperback)

Any references to historical events, real people, or real places are used fictitiously. Names, characters, and situations in this book are purely the product of the author's imagination.

Cover design by - Thomas M. Ransome

Interior layout by Thomas M. Ransome

First Edition, 2024

Published by Thomas M. Ransome

The Wealth Game

Thomas M. Ransome

Table of Contents

The Wealth Game

Introduction

The Wealth Game is not just a book; it's a blueprint for navigating the intricate world of finance, a world often perceived as a complex maze where only a few people actually win. This book is designed to expose you to the truth that - like any game -the financial world is made up of levels, each with its own set of rules and strategies.

When it comes to money, it often appears as though only a select few know how to play this game effectively. They are the 1% who seem to conquer level after level, accumulating wealth and success. Their secret? A deep understanding of the rules and the wisdom to use those rules to their advantage. However, these rules, which should be universal, are often unknown or overlooked by the majority. This gap in knowledge and application is what creates the divide between the financial elite and the rest.

The Wealth Game is your guide to bridge this divide. It's crafted to lay a foundational understanding of money management and how to advance through the levels of financial mastery. This book is more than a collection of financial advice; it's the accelerant to spark a movement. A movement of wealth builders, visionaries, and change-makers who are ready to attract and gather the resources needed to fuel their visions and impact the world around them.

As you go through this book, I want you to see the world through the lens of potential and opportunity. This is a call to action for you, fellow wealth builder, to embrace the vision God has placed in your heart and to _actively_ work towards realizing it. It's an invitation to shift your mindset to where financial literacy is not just about personal gain but about empowering yourself and others and making a lasting difference.

Each chapter of this book is a step forward in this game. From establishing the right mindset to mastering the skills of budgeting, saving, and investing, you will gain insights into ascending the levels of financial success. You'll learn not just to play the game but to master it, moving from basic financial understanding to sophisticated investment strategies. As you delve into the pages of this book, be prepared for a transformation. You'll be equipped not only with knowledge but with practical tools and strategies to navigate the financial world. This book is designed to grow your financial literacy, enabling you to make informed decisions that align with your vision and values.

While this book contains knowledge and wisdom for financial success, this book should not take the place of specific and tailored financial advice from a financial professional. Coming from the world of banking and finance, I will always stand on this one piece of advice: no matter what you hear, no matter how good or amazing it may seem, consult with your team of financial professionals. And if you don't have a team... build one. The components of that team? I put them in here, too!

So, read on and absorb within these pages, not simply reading it, but putting it into action. Master the game of wealth and build something that lasts for generations. Remember, this is about more than just accumulating wealth; it's about creating a legacy of knowledge, empowerment, and purposeful living. Your journey to financial mastery begins now – get locked in, get ready, and join me as we learn and grow together!

Chapter One:
The Time is Now

Welcome to the game of wealth. In this game, you are not just a bystander; you are an active player, making moves that shape your financial future. Too long now, you have sat by and lived a life of hope. Hoping to make a lot of money. Hoping for a new job that gives you that six-figure salary for which you have been waiting. Hoping that a lifestyle of luxury and leaving a legacy to your children comes along and finds you. Hoping and waiting. But this game doesn't find people waiting on the sidelines and carry them to the finish line. There are no cheat codes. Even lottery winners find themselves broke financially and relationally. Or worse.

But that doesn't have to continue to be your place. You can step onto the playing field, make an impact, and build wealth that will transcend your generation and even beyond the generation of your children's children. This book serves as your guide, offering insights and strategies to navigate the game effectively. So, let's begin our journey.

Understanding the Game Board

Think of wealth building as a board game laid out before us. Each player starts from a unique position, but the goal is universal: to navigate this board with wisdom and strategy. This game isn't about accumulating wealth for its own sake. It's about creating wealth with a purpose, wealth that can have a lasting impact on the world around us. Why is it crucial to start playing this game now? Let's examine some compelling statistics and reasons that underscore the urgency.

Three Undeniable Truths

Firstly, let's consider the significant wealth gap in black and brown communities. Numerous studies have highlighted that these households generally possess a lower median net worth compared to their counterparts. Simply put: these families own less than their counterparts. This gap is more than a statistical gap; it reflects an incredible history of missed opportunities and unfulfilled potential. It's a reminder of the barriers that need dismantling - whether physical or mental - and the role financial literacy and empowerment can play in this process.

Secondly, the lack of basic financial education in these communities is profoundly concerning. This isn't just about inequality; it's about an opportunity for empowerment. Financial literacy is a powerful tool. It transforms lives, shifting individuals and entire families from financial uncertainty to security, from dependence to independence. By embracing financial education, we can ignite a transformation that extends beyond individuals and families to entire communities.

Thirdly, there's a noticeable trend of entrepreneurship and wealth creation within these communities. The most common and tested way to create wealth is to own a business. And almost anyone can own any type of business. You have to simply make a decision and go do it! This isn't a simple glimpse of hope; it's a testament to what's possible. It shows that the times are changing, and financial success is within reach. This shows a break from the past, offering us concrete pathways to bridge the wealth gap and create a legacy of prosperity for ourselves, our families, and our communities.

Why Should You Start Now?

1. **Empowerment through Financial Independence:** Financial independence is about more than just money. It's about the freedom to make choices based on what you truly desire, not just what you need. This independence is liberating. It allows you to live on your own terms, pursue your passions, and make decisions that align with your personal values and aspirations.

2. **Ability to Impact and Uplift the Community:** Your journey to building wealth is not just a personal achievement; it's an opportunity to effect positive change in your community. When you succeed financially, you set an example. You become a source of inspiration and a catalyst for growth. Your success has the power to uplift others, creating a ripple effect of empowerment and opportunity.

3. **Greater Control Over Personal and Professional Life:** Financial stability opens a world of choices. It allows you to pursue a career you love, not just one that pays the bills. This control extends beyond your professional life; it encompasses all areas, enabling you to make choices that resonate with your personal goals and lifestyle aspirations.

4. **Legacy Building for Future Generations:** Your financial journey is about creating a foundation for the future. It's about setting the stage for the next generation, ensuring they have the resources and knowledge to build upon your success. This legacy is a powerful motivator, driving you to create not just wealth but a lasting impact.

5. **Closing the Wealth Gap:** Every step you take towards building your wealth contributes to a larger cause – narrowing the systemic wealth gap. It's a step towards creating a more equitable financial landscape, one where opportunities for prosperity are accessible to all, regardless of background or circumstance.

The Game of Strategy

In this game, every move you make is critical. Each action, whether saving a little extra, investing wisely, or reducing debt, is part of your strategic plan for a brighter financial future. This game is about making informed decisions, understanding the impact of each choice, and navigating the path to wealth with intention and purpose. This game requires intentional, educated, and focused activities to really be successful. As we move deeper into this book, we'll explore the essential strategies and habits for winning this game. We'll discuss how to cultivate a vision for your life, leverage your personal 'machine,' master money management, and much more.

Each chapter is a step towards not just building wealth, but doing so with significance and influence, and the time to start playing seriously is now. This isn't just about financial gain; it's about a journey of personal growth, resource management, and community impact. It's about transforming your relationship with money and understanding its role not just in your life but in the broader context of society. Each chapter of this book will equip you with the knowledge and tools you need to grow personally and professionally, improve your money management, and maximize your impact on society.

Remember, in the wealth game, every decision, no matter how small, contributes to your overall strategy. From understanding the basics of personal finance to exploring advanced investment strategies, you'll learn how to play this game like a pro. It's about playing the long game, making moves that compound over time to create a legacy of wealth and impact. So, are you ready to take control and make your move? The time is now, and your journey towards financial empowerment and freedom starts here. Let's take this first step together and start changing the game!

Thomas M. Ransome

Chapter Two:
Victory Requires Vision

If the first chapter was about understanding the urgency of starting this game, then this chapter is about defining your strategy through the game. Just as every skilled player needs a strategy to win, every wealth builder needs a strategy and vision to guide their financial journey. In this chapter, we will explore the power of vision in shaping your path to financial success.

Crafting Your Vision: The Blueprint of Success

Think of your vision as the blueprint of your financial game. It's a vivid, detailed picture of where you want to go, what you want to achieve, and who you want to become. A vision is not just a dream; it is a strategic plan that guides your every move. A vision helps you live narrow, eliminating the unnecessary and focusing on the essential.

Your vision should encompass both your personal and financial aspirations. It's about integrating your life goals with your financial targets. Imagine your ideal life in detail. Where are you living? What kind of work are you doing? What impact are you making in your community? Now, align these images with your financial goals. How much wealth do you need to turn this vision into reality? What kind of financial stability will support your life goals?

Your vision acts as your North Star, guiding you through every decision and challenge. It helps you stay focused and motivated, especially when the game gets tough. Your vision reminds you of why you started this journey and what you're playing for.

The Power of Vision: The Foundation of Victory

A well-defined vision is not just a nice-to-have; it's a must-have in your wealth-building journey. Let's delve into the benefits of having a clear, empowering vision.

1. **Clarity in Decision-Making:** With a clear vision, every financial decision becomes easier. You will know which opportunities align with your goals and which ones to pass up. This clarity saves you from distractions and keeps you focused on moves that advance you towards your goals.
2. **Stronger Focus and Dedication**: A compelling vision keeps you driven, especially during challenging times. When obstacles arise, as they inevitably will in this game, your vision becomes a source of strength and resilience. It reminds you of the end game, helping you stay locked in on your "why" and maintain your focus and dedication.
3. **Enhanced Motivation During Challenges:** In life, setbacks are not losses; they are lessons. And the same is true in the game of wealth. A powerful vision helps you see these setbacks in the right perspective, fueling your motivation to

overcome challenges and continue moving forward. Don't see the mistakes or missteps as losses; view them as lessons, learning what you need to in order to be successful the next time around.

Creating Your Vision: A Step-by-Step Guide

Now, let's walk through the steps of creating a personal vision that will empower your wealth building mission:

1. **Reflect on Personal Values and Goals:** Start by reflecting on what truly matters to you. What are your core values? What are your life goals? Understanding these will help you craft a vision that is deeply personal and meaningful.

2. **Research and Find Role Models:** Look for inspiration in stories of others who have achieved similar goals. These role models can provide valuable insights and serve as examples of what's possible. Study their journey, learn from their strategies, and see how they aligned their vision with their actions.

3. **Create a Vision Board or Written Statement:** A vision board is a powerful tool to visualize your goals. Collect images and words that represent your ideal life and financial aspirations. Alternatively, write a detailed statement describing your vision. Or... DO BOTH! The key is to make them as vivid and specific as possible. It must be something that excites you every time you look at it!

4. **Set Measurable and Achievable Goals:** Break down your vision into achievable goals. What steps do you need to take this year, this month, or even this week to move closer to your vision? Setting measurable goals gives you a clear roadmap and milestones to celebrate along the way.

5. **Regularly Review and Adapt the Vision:** Your vision is not set in stone. As you execute your strategy, your understanding and circumstances might change. Regularly review and adjust your vision to ensure it remains relevant and inspiring.

Making Strategic Moves

With your vision in place, every move you make in this game now becomes more strategic and intentional. Your financial decisions – from saving and investing to spending and giving – all align with your vision. This alignment ensures that your actions not only propel you forward but also keep you true to your personal values and life goals. If you fail to consult your vision daily, you will find that your activity doesn't match your goals. Make sure that your actions align with your vision every step of the way!

Commitment and Adaptability

As a player in the game of wealth, it is imperative that you commit to your vision and remain adaptable at the same time. It is easy to get locked to a way of doing things or stuck on one perspective. From technological changes to your own personal wants and desires to the social and economic environment... the game's landscape will change. New opportunities and challenges will arise, which means that your vision will be necessary to help you navigate these opportunities and challenges with confidence and purpose.

What Lies Ahead

Remember, crafting and following a vision is not a one-time task; it's an ongoing process. It requires continuous reflection, learning, and adaptation. Your vision is your compass in all of this, guiding you towards victory – a life of financial success, the creation of a multigenerational legacy, and personal fulfillment.

As we move to the next chapters, get ready to build on this foundation, exploring how to power your 'machine,' master money management, save strategically, manage credit wisely, and unleash your inner investor. With each chapter, I want to bring you closer to realizing your vision and equip you with the skills and knowledge to win. And remember: winning in this game is not just about the wealth you accumulate; it's about the life you create and the impact you make.

Thomas M. Ransome

Chapter Three:
The Power of Your Machine

Welcome to the third level of The Wealth Game, where we begin transforming your perspective and amplifying your potential. In this chapter, we focus on one of the most pivotal aspects of the game: understanding and harnessing the power of your personal 'machine.' This 'machine' isn't a physical entity; it's a metaphor for your career or business – the primary vehicle through which you generate income and build wealth.

Understanding Your 'Machine'

Your 'machine' is your means of production, the source of your financial energy. It's what you use to create value in the marketplace, whether that's through your job, your business, or your investments. This chapter is about shifting from an employee mindset, where you're a cog in someone else's machine, to a business owner mindset, where you control your own machine. No, you don't need to own a business to win this game, although entrepreneurs generally have greater odds to create the wealth they desire because they have more control over how much their machine earns. An employee can do it too!

As an employee working for someone else, your ability to earn is limited by someone else's determination of what they will pay you for the job you do. But, you can have a business mindset even as you work for someone else. Every business owner understands (or at least they should) that you are paid based on the value provided. It's the very principle that allows luxury cars to have higher price tags than regular cars. Both have wheels, windows, and doors, but the value that the luxury brands provide is perceived to be greater and therefore worth more. So people pay top dollar for high end brand names even though their utility is the same as a non-luxury brand.

You as an employee can increase your pay by increasing your value to the marketplace. This may not happen with your current employer, simply demanding a raise because you do more than your job requires. However, you might look outside to a competing firm who may pay you more because of all that you do for your current firm. How? By communicating what you do and the outcome it produces for your current employer. In business, this is called sales. As an employee, it's called putting it on your resume and talking about it in an interview. What certifications can you get? What activities do you do outside of work for fun? What are some of your hobbies? What skills have you acquired at previous places of business? College? High school? All of these are "value-added items" that can improve how attractive you (the product) look to an employer. Increase your value, increase your income, and increase the output of your machine.

However, there are only a few professions or careers that can outpace a profitable, well-organized business. Entrepreneurs have so much control over their earning potential that they can increase their machine's output rapidly by simply adjusting how they manage their income. A good business will have low costs and high revenue earned, leading to a wide profit margin. It should be legally structured to give you the best tax benefits. Ultimately, a good business will be something that can be passed down to the next generation, should that be part of your vision plan. But, regardless of how you choose to build your wealth, you need to have the proper mindset!

The Employee vs. Business Owner Mindset

1. **Employee Mindset:** This mindset is about trading time for money. You perform tasks as assigned and receive a paycheck in return. While this can provide stability, it often limits your income potential and control over your financial future. The focus here should be on acquiring skills that are attractive to employers in your chosen career field

2. **Business Owner Mindset:** This mindset is about creating value and leveraging resources (time, money, skills) to generate income. Here, your focus shifts from earning a wage to building an entity that works for you, increasing your potential for income and wealth. Your mindset should be centered around decreasing business costs, increasing revenue earned, and legally positioning your business to be an asset during a wealth transition.

The Benefits of a Good 'Machine'

Let's explore the benefits of building and operating a well-oiled 'machine.'

1. **Increased Earning Potential:** Unlike a job where your income is typically fixed or incrementally increased, a business can

scale. As you grow your 'machine,' your earning potential multiplies.

2. **Autonomy and Self-direction:** Owning your 'machine' means making decisions that align with your personal and financial goals. This autonomy allows you to steer your career or business in the direction you desire.

3. **Personal Growth and Skill Development:** Running your own 'machine' requires a diverse skill set and continuous learning. This journey of personal and professional development can be incredibly rewarding.

Building Your 'Machine'

Building your 'machine' is not an overnight task. It requires careful planning, consistent effort, and a willingness to learn and adapt. Here's a step-by-step guide to building a 'machine' that reflects your value, natural gifts, and acquired skills.

1. **Identify Personal Strengths and Passions:** Start by understanding what you're good at and what you enjoy doing. Your 'machine' should be built around your strengths and passions, as this alignment will drive your motivation and creativity.

2. **Gain Relevant Education and Skills**: No matter what your 'machine' is, it will require specific skills and knowledge. Invest in education – formal or informal – to build the expertise you need to succeed.

3. **Seek Mentorship and Networking Opportunities:** Learning from those who have successfully built their 'machines' can

accelerate your journey. Seek out mentors and network within your industry to gain insights and open doors to new opportunities.

4. **Develop a Business or Career Plan:** Map out a plan for your 'machine.' This plan should include your business model (how you'll make money), your target market, and your strategies for growth.

5. **Continuously Evaluate and Adjust the 'Machine':** Your 'machine' should evolve as you grow and as market conditions change. Regularly assess its performance and make adjustments as needed.

The Journey of Building Your 'Machine'

Building your 'machine' is a journey filled with challenges and triumphs. It's about taking what you have – your skills, knowledge, and passions – and turning them into something valuable in the marketplace. It's about moving beyond the limitations of a job and embracing the potential of entrepreneurship or career growth.

Lessons from Successful 'Machines'

To understand the power of a well-built 'machine,' let's look at some case studies (hypothetical for illustrative purposes):

- **Case Study 1:** Sarah, a graphic designer, transitioned from a full-time job to freelancing and then to owning her design agency. Her journey involved honing her skills, building a client base, and gradually scaling her business. Today, her 'machine' not only provides a substantial income but also allows her the freedom to choose projects that align with her creative vision.

- **Case Study 2:** Alex, an IT professional, used his expertise to develop a software solution for small businesses. Starting as a side project, it grew into a profitable company. Alex's 'machine' combined his technical skills with a gap he identified in the market, resulting in a successful business venture.

Continuous Learning and Adaptation

Building your 'machine' requires a commitment to continuous learning and adaptation. The market is constantly evolving, and so should your 'machine.' Stay updated with industry trends, invest in developing new skills, and be open to pivoting your strategies when necessary. Building your 'machine' also involves balancing risk and opportunity. That means stepping out of your comfort zone and facing uncertainties. However, with careful planning and strategic execution, the potential rewards – both financial and personal – can be significant.

No matter what you do, you need to be able to shift directions to remain in demand and valuable. One example of this is the rapid development of artificial intelligence and its various applications. Either you are innovative enough to create a new application or you are adaptable enough to master an existing one. Both will lead you to a place where you are in demand because you can teach or train others.

A Catalyst for Wealth

Remember that your 'machine' is more than just a source of income. It's a catalyst for wealth creation, a tool for shaping your financial future, and a reflection of your unique value and capabilities.

You must manage this well, continuing to build and add to the value it provides. Whether a career or a business, you must be focused on improving and developing who you are, what value you provide, and what impact you make. This will allow you to increase your income and accelerate your wealth accumulation.

In the upcoming chapters, we are going to build on this foundation. We will explore how to master money management, save strategically, manage credit wisely, and become a savvy investor. An optimized machine produces massive income and that income has potential that requires purpose and a plan. I am going to show you how to give your income what it needs to maximize that potential! The power of your 'machine' is immense, and with the right approach, it can lead you to success in executing your wealth plan!

Chapter Four:
Master Money Management

As we advance to the fourth level of The Wealth Game, we focus on a skill that is fundamental to your success: Mastering Money Management. This chapter is not about complex financial strategies; it's about the basics of budgeting and cash flow management. Every financial planner and investment strategist will tell you that none of those advanced levels are available to those who cannot master the basic skill of budgeting. Your finances are the lifeblood of your wealth building strategy and without a good management system, you will never have enough money to advance any further. This skill is the essential tool you need to ensure that your hard-earned money is working effectively for you, laying the groundwork for long-term wealth accumulation.

Understanding the Role of Budgeting

Your budget is your game plan. It's a detailed blueprint of how you allocate your resources (income) to achieve your goals (expenses, savings, investments). A well-structured budget gives you control over your finances and is a critical step towards financial freedom. A budget isn't a constraint; it's a roadmap that guides your financial journey. It helps you prioritize your spending, ensuring that your money is being used effectively to reach your goals. Understanding and managing your cash flow – the money flowing in and out of your hands – is crucial. It requires ensuring that you're not only living within your means but also saving for the future.

The Benefits of a Good Budgeting System

A robust budgeting system is a powerful tool. Let's explore the benefits:

1. **Financial Stability and Peace of Mind:** A budget provides a sense of security. Knowing that your finances are under control can significantly reduce stress and anxiety related to money.
2. **Efficient Resource Allocation:** Budgeting helps you allocate your resources efficiently. It ensures that important expenses are covered, debts are paid, and savings goals are on track.
3. **Foundation for Wealth Accumulation:** Effective budgeting lays the foundation for building wealth. It allows you to identify and capitalize on opportunities to save and invest, accelerating your wealth accumulation.

Mastering Budgeting: A Step-by-Step Guide

Mastering budgeting is a journey that requires commitment and consistency. Here's how to develop and maintain an effective budgeting system.

1. **Track Income and Expenses:** The first step is to understand where your money comes from and where it goes. Track your income and categorize your expenses (necessities, luxuries, savings, debts) to get a clear picture of your financial situation.

2. **Set Realistic Budgeting Goals:** Based on your income and expenses, set realistic and achievable budgeting goals. These goals should align with your short-term and long-term financial objectives.

3. **Prioritize Essential Expenses:** Ensure that your budget covers essential expenses first – housing, utilities, food, health care, and debt repayment. This prioritization ensures that your basic needs are always met.

4. **Regularly Review and Adjust the Budget:** Your budget should be a living document, regularly reviewed and adjusted. As your income, expenses, and financial goals change, so should your budget.

5. **Utilize Budgeting Tools and Apps:** Technology can be a great ally in budgeting. Use apps and tools to track your expenses, set reminders for bill payments, and monitor your progress towards your financial goals.

The Psychology of Spending: Understanding Your Habits

Mastering money management isn't just about mastering numbers; it's also about understanding and mastering your spending habits. Are you an impulsive buyer? Do you spend more when you're stressed or happy? Understanding the psychology behind your spending can help you make more conscious financial decisions. Your vision may be your north star, but your habits are the transportation. You will only go as far as the habits you cultivate. You will only cultivate good habits if you have the right mindset.

Creating a Savings Mindset

An integral part of mastering money management is developing a savings mindset. This means prioritizing saving over spending and viewing savings as a regular expense in your budget.

1. **Emergency Fund: Your Financial Safety Net:** Building an emergency fund should be a top priority. This fund acts as a buffer against unexpected expenses, reducing the need to rely on credit or disrupt your investment plans.
2. **Short-term and Long-term Savings Goals:** Apart from an emergency fund, your budget should also cater to other savings goals – be it a down payment for a house, a vacation fund, or retirement savings.

Managing Debt Wisely

How you manage debt can significantly impact your financial health. It's about striking a balance – using debt as a tool for building wealth while avoiding the pitfalls of excessive debt.

1. **Good Debt vs. Bad Debt:** Understand the difference between good debt (that which helps you build wealth, like a mortgage) and bad debt (high-interest consumer debt). Your budget should prioritize paying off bad debt while strategically managing good debt.

2. **Debt Repayment Strategies:** Incorporate effective debt repayment strategies into your budget. Whether it's the snowball method (paying off smaller debts first) or the avalanche method (paying off high-interest debts first), choose a strategy that aligns with your financial situation.

Advanced Budgeting Techniques

As you progress in mastering money management, explore advanced budgeting techniques. These might include zero-based budgeting (allocating every dollar of income), envelope system (allocating cash for different spending categories), or automated savings and investment plans.

The Key to Winning 'The Wealth Game'

Mastering money management is a critical skill in this game, especially if you want to live in a place of abundance. It's about taking control of your finances, making informed decisions, living a disciplined life, and setting the stage for wealth accumulation. As we continue, this foundational principle will feed all other principles. Without a strong money management plan and process in place, you will fail in your efforts to supercharge your savings, optimize your credit, and invest strategically. I won't lie to you. This will be your most difficult task... but if you win here, you will win everywhere else!

Chapter Five:
Be a Super Saver

Building on the crucial skills of budgeting and money management from Chapter 4, we now ascend to the next level in The Wealth Game - becoming a Super Saver. This chapter isn't just about putting aside money; it's about cultivating a mindset of saving that transforms your financial future. Here, we explore the art of saving with a focus on creating a strong foundation for financial stability and growth.

The Essence of a Savings Mindset

A savings mindset is your armor. It's a perspective that prioritizes accumulating wealth over immediate gratification. It is embracing delayed gratification as functional to attain a life of abundance. This mindset is crucial because it shapes every financial decision you make, turning saving from a chore into a strategic and rewarding part of your game plan.

1. **Delayed Gratification, The Superpower of Savers**: Embracing delayed gratification is central to developing a savings mindset. It's about recognizing that forgoing short-term pleasures can lead to long-term benefits and financial security.
2. **Savings as a Habit, Not an Option:** Transforming saving into a habit means treating it like a non-negotiable part of your budget. Just as you allocate funds for rent or groceries, savings should have its dedicated place in your financial plan. Automation is essential to making this a habit.

The Benefits of Learning the Skill of Saving Money

Developing the skill of saving money has far-reaching benefits in this game

1. **Financial Security for Unexpected Events:** An emergency fund is your financial lifeline. It's a cushion that protects you from life's unforeseen financial shocks, be it job loss, medical emergencies, or urgent home repairs.
2. **Resources for Significant Life Events:** Saving enables you to accumulate funds for significant life events, such as buying a home, funding education, or enjoying a well-deserved retirement.
3. **Increased Sense of Control Over Finances:** Regular saving enhances your sense of control over your finances. It reduces stress and anxiety about money, giving you peace of mind.

Building a Strong Savings Strategy: Essential Steps

You want to master saving as a habit and start building your wealth?

Follow these essential steps:

1. **Set Clear Saving Goals:** Define what you're saving for. Whether it's an emergency fund, a house, education, retirement, or a dream vacation, having clear goals gives your saving efforts direction and purpose. Resources without purpose will always end up leaving your hands in ways you don't want.

2. **Automate Savings:** Automation is a powerful tool in building a savings habit. Set up automatic transfers to your savings account each time you receive your paycheck. This 'set and forget' approach ensures that you're consistently saving without the temptation to spend. This is your game changer!

3. **Cut Unnecessary Expenses:** Revisit your budget from Chapter 4 and identify areas where you can reduce spending. Redirect these funds into your savings. Even small adjustments can add up over time. Check your vision against your expenditures. Do they line up with how you see your life? What if you delayed that expense until you finances were optimized? How would that impact your wealth building results?

4. **Increase Income Streams:** To boost your savings, consider ways to increase your income. This could be through a side hustle, freelancing, or investing in skills that lead to higher-paying job opportunities. Embracing delayed gratification is essential to winning here. Don't make more and spend more. Make more and save more!

5. **Regularly Monitor and Celebrate Progress:** Keep track of your savings progress and celebrate milestones. This positive reinforcement encourages you to continue saving and reinforces the savings habit. Plan for money set aside to treat yourself! Diets have cheat days and so do budgets! Set aside some funds to reward yourself for hitting your savings goals.

Overcoming the Challenges in Saving

While saving is a crucial skill, it's not without its challenges. Economic fluctuations, lifestyle inflation, and personal emergencies can disrupt your saving plans. To navigate these challenges, remain flexible and adaptable in your approach. Reassess and adjust your saving goals as needed, always keeping your long-term vision in sight. When you study your vision, do so with your budget and your savings goals. Finances are fuel that gets you from where you are now into the future that you have seen before you. Cars have different fuel consumption based on environmental conditions. Think highway miles vs city miles. Adjust. Adapt. Be flexible. And then get back on track to each goal that you have.

The Role of Emergency Funds

An emergency fund is a cornerstone of a Super Saver's strategy. Aim to save at least 6 to 12 months' worth of living expenses. This figure used to be 3 - 6 months, however, after the events of 2020 and the COVID-19 pandemic, having more is better should there be some sort of long term emergency. This fund should be easily accessible and separate from your other savings or investment accounts.

Short-Term vs. Long-Term Savings

Balancing short-term and long-term savings is key. Short-term savings caters to immediate or near-future needs, like a vacation or a new vehicle, while long-term savings are for goals several years away, like retirement or purchasing a home. Each has its place in your overall financial strategy and should be utilized when necessary.

Advanced Saving Strategies

As you progress in growing your savings and building your wealth, explore advanced saving strategies. These might include high-yield savings accounts, certificates of deposit (CDs), or government bonds. These instruments can offer higher returns on your savings, accelerating your progress towards your financial goals. Understanding the tools that are available to you in your wealth building journey is key to using the right strategy to accomplish your goals. Don't use short-term tools for long-term money and vice versa. Match the tool to the purpose of the savings strategy and find massive success.

Savings should be a part of your broader wealth-building strategy. It's a foundation upon which you can build investments. Once your emergency fund and short-term goals are funded, redirect excess savings into investment vehicles that offer higher growth potential. We are going to speak more about investing in a later chapter, but this right here is gold. Saving is good, but improving how well your money works for you is better.

Being a Super Saver in The Wealth Game is about more than accumulating money; it's about building a secure, stable, and prosperous financial future. It's a commitment to your long-term goals and a testament to your discipline and foresight. It is embracing delayed gratification for the purpose of hitting the far greater future goals of your vision over the short-sighted wants that slowly eat away at your finances.

Each step in this journey is interconnected, with your savings habits providing another of the foundations upon which you can build significant wealth. It requires discipline, patience, and a steadfast commitment to your financial goals. But the rewards – financial security, peace of mind, and the ability to achieve your dreams – are well worth the effort!

Chapter Six:
Crush Your Credit

Having fortified our saving strategies in Chapter 5, we now transition to another vital aspect of "The Wealth Game" – mastering the art of credit management. This chapter is dedicated to understanding, building, and effectively utilizing credit. Credit, when managed wisely, can be a powerful tool in your financial arsenal, helping you advance in the game.

Understanding the Power of Credit

Credit is a strategic piece of building wealth that, when played correctly, can significantly enhance your position. It's not just about borrowing money. That's a juvenile way of understanding credit. Instead, it is about using additional financial resources and tools in order to add assets to your bottom line. An asset is something that has and holds value. A house has value. A car has value. Jewelry. Life insurance. There is a value attached to them. And the best kind of asset is a cash flowing asset... an asset that makes you money. Rental property. Business. Investments. When you manage debt well -

borrowing money with purpose and paying it back properly - you are building a reputation in the financial world that you're trustworthy and capable of managing debt responsibly.

1. **Credit as a Financial Lever:** Good credit opens doors to financial opportunities that can be game-changers. It allows you to leverage funds for significant investments like buying a home or starting a business.
2. **The Cost of Credit:** Understanding interest rates and how they impact the cost of borrowing is crucial. Good credit can lead to lower interest rates, saving you significant amounts of money over time.

The Benefits of Strong Personal and Business Credit

Building strong personal and business credit comes with substantial benefits in this game:

1. **Access to More Financial Opportunities:** Good credit often equates to access to better financial products and opportunities, including lower interest rates on loans and credit cards. Good credit opens more doors.
2. **Lower Interest Rates and Better Loan Terms:** A strong credit score can lead to more favorable loan terms. This can mean lower interest rates, which translates into lower costs over the life of the loan. Lower costs mean more profit, which means faster growth of wealth through savings and investing
3. **Leverage in Purchasing Assets:** Good credit provides leverage in purchasing assets like real estate or investing in business opportunities. It can be the difference between securing funding for an investment or missing out.

Building a Strong Credit Score

Building a strong credit score is a critical part of a credit strategy in building wealth. Here's how to approach it:

1. **Understand Your Credit Score:** Familiarize yourself with how credit scores are calculated. The five key factors are payment history, credit utilization, length of credit history, new credit, and credit mix.
2. **Timely Payment of Bills:** Always pay your bills on time. Late payments can significantly harm your credit score.
3. **Manage Credit Card Usage:** Keep your credit card balances low. High balances can negatively impact your credit utilization ratio, a key factor in determining your credit score.
4. **Diversify Types of Credit:** A mix of different types of credit (like revolving credit and installment loans) can positively affect your credit score.
5. **Regularly Review Credit Reports:** Check your credit reports regularly for errors or fraudulent activities. Report any inaccuracies immediately.

Rebuilding Credit

But what if you didn't get it right from the beginning? If you're like me, you learned about credit or are learning about credit after hurting your credit. For those who have experienced financial hardships leading to poor credit, the journey of rebuilding credit is essential.

Here's how to start:

1. **Assess Your Credit Situation:** Obtain your credit report to understand where you stand. Identify the areas that need improvement, such as outstanding debts or errors.
2. **Develop a Plan to Address Issues:** Create a plan to tackle issues like outstanding debts. Consider strategies like debt consolidation or negotiating with creditors.
3. **Establish New Credit Habits:** Start building positive credit habits. This can involve small, manageable steps like using a secured credit card responsibly.
4. **Be Patient and Persistent:** Rebuilding credit takes time and consistency. Stay committed to your plan and be patient as your credit score gradually improves.

The Major Credit Bureaus: Their Role in Your Credit Score

Understanding the role of the major credit bureaus is crucial in managing and rebuilding credit. These bureaus collect and maintain the data that forms your credit report, which in turn influences your credit score.

1. **Equifax:** One of the three major credit bureaus, Equifax collects and aggregates information on over 800 million individual consumers and more than 88 million businesses worldwide.
2. **Experian:** Experian is another leading credit bureau that gathers and maintains information on millions of consumers and businesses globally, helping to inform credit decisions.

3. **TransUnion:** The third major credit bureau, TransUnion, also collects and stores credit information and is known for its role in offering credit protection and identity theft prevention services.

Regularly monitoring your credit reports from these bureaus is vital. It allows you to track your progress, identify areas for improvement, and catch potential errors or fraudulent activities.

Strategies for Managing Debt Levels

Effective debt management is a critical aspect of credit mastery. This involves understanding your debt-to-income ratio, prioritizing high-interest debts, and avoiding unnecessary new debts.

1. **Understand Your Debt-to-Income Ratio:** This ratio measures your monthly debt payments against your income. Keeping this ratio low is key to maintaining good credit. To get this number, take the total dollar amount of the monthly payments of your credit obligations and divide that number by your monthly before tax income. This percentage is the amount of debt you have compared to your income. 35% or less is a great place to be. Anything higher and you need to get to work dropping your debt.
2. **Prioritize High-Interest Debts:** Focus on paying off high-interest debts first, as they cost you the most over time. This is a strategy that can work, especially if you don't have a lot of smaller debts like credit cards.
3. **Avoid Unnecessary New Debts:** Be cautious about taking on new debts. Evaluate the necessity and impact of any new debt on your overall financial health. Remember: delayed gratification is key for your financial success.

Credit Mastery is Wealth Building Power

Mastering credit in The Wealth Game is about understanding its power, building a strong credit profile, and using credit strategically to advance your financial goals. Whether you're building credit from scratch, strengthening your current credit standing, or rebuilding from financial setbacks, the process of credit mastery requires knowledge, discipline, and strategic action. Remember, credit is not just a tool for borrowing; it's a strategic asset that - when managed wisely - can significantly boost your journey towards financial success and stability!

Chapter Seven:
Unleashing the Investor

This chapter is about advancing to the highest level of building wealth: investing. It's time to dive into the realm where your savings and credit proficiency come together to create opportunities for your money to grow independently, marking a significant transition from earning wealth to multiplying wealth.

Investing in 'The Wealth Game'

In this game of wealth, investing is like advancing to and playing on the highest level. Here, the decisions become more strategic and the potential rewards become greater. Investing is the process of using your money to acquire assets that offer potential profitable returns through income, value appreciation, or both. Simply put: investing is putting your money to work for you!

1. **Beyond Saving and Earning:** While saving is about accumulating and preserving money and earning is about exchanging your time and skills for money, investing is about making your money work for you. You will find that **_ownership_** is the best and most tested way to build wealth. When you invest, you purchase some (or all) of a business, commodity, or real estate in order to benefit financially.

2. **Compound Interest is a Game Changer:** Understanding the power of compound interest is crucial. It's the process where the interest you earn generates its interest, exponentially increasing your wealth over time. The more you earn, the more it earns, and the more you earn, and the more it earns... you get the picture!

The Benefits of Investing

Investing brings massive benefits for your wealth building strategy:

1. **Potential for Passive Income:** Investments can generate income streams, such as dividends or rental income, providing you with money that doesn't require active work.

2. **Diversification of Wealth:** Investing allows you to spread your money across different assets, reducing risk and stabilizing your financial portfolio.

3. **Benefit from Economic Growth**: By investing in stocks or businesses, you can benefit from economic growth, as these investments tend to increase in value over time.

Strategic Portfolio Building

One of the most important things to understand about investing is that it is generally a long term strategy and not a short term one. Your investment goals and strategies should have longer time frames for completion. Think years and decades, not weeks and months. Because of this forward looking approach to wealth building, investing requires that your immediate needs are covered. Low debt to income ratios (below 35%), emergency fund needs met (6-12 months saved), and strong disposable cash flow (10-20% monthly). That 10-20% can now be placed in an investment strategy that will create exponential growth.

Here's how to approach building a portfolio:

1. **Assess Your Financial Situation and Goals:** Before you start investing, assess your financial health. Ensure you have a solid foundation – a well-managed budget, an emergency fund, and manageable debt levels. Review your vision and make sure that you have achieved all of the goals mentioned in prior chapters.

2. **Understand Your Risk Tolerance:** Every investment carries some level of risk. Understanding your risk tolerance – how much risk you are willing and able to take – is vital in choosing suitable investments. This is generally determined by your investment purpose and goals. Retirement is more time bound, meaning that the younger you are the more risk you can take. The older you get, you move from aggressive to conservative investments. Income investing is less time bound and more results oriented, meaning you will only invest in assets that will produce income regularly.

3. **Start Small and Diversify:** Begin with small investments and diversify your portfolio. Diversification – spreading your investments across various asset types – can reduce risk. This is an underrated step that many investors miss. The more

diverse you are, the more you can withstand economic issues. Remember: diversify over time to have the most impact.

4. **Regularly Review and Adjust Your Portfolio:** Just like any other aspect of this game, your investment portfolio requires regular review and adjustments based on performance and changing financial goals. Always look at your vision and ensure that you are meeting the standards and expectations you set for yourself.

Investment Options: Exploring the Different Types

There are various investment options available, each with its characteristics and levels of risk and return.

1. **Real Estate:** Investing in property can provide rental income and potential value appreciation. It's a tangible asset and can be a stable investment in a well-balanced portfolio.
2. **Stocks and Bonds:** Stocks give you a share in a company's ownership and potential dividends, while bonds are like loans to companies or governments, earning you interest over time.
3. **Investment Funds (Mutual Funds, ETFs):** These funds pool money from many investors to invest in a diversified portfolio of stocks, bonds, or other assets.
4. **Businesses:** Investing in a business, whether starting your own or funding others (like startups), can offer substantial returns but also carries higher risks.
5. **Commodities:** These include physical assets like gold, oil, or agricultural products. They can be volatile but can also serve as a hedge against inflation.

Investing and Credit

Your credit health, as discussed in Chapter 6, can play a role in your investing journey. Good credit can provide opportunities for leveraging – using borrowed money to increase the potential return of an investment.

1. **Investment Loans:** A strong credit score can help you secure loans for investment purposes at favorable terms.
2. **Real Estate Mortgages:** Good credit is essential for obtaining mortgages for real estate investments.

The Path to Exponential Growth

A powerful strategy is the reinvestment of your profits, a method that serves as the engine driving your wealth growth. Reinvesting isn't just about pouring your returns back into the market; it's a deliberate action to leave your gains in the account and fuel the expansion of your financial portfolio. Reinvestment is all about delayed gratification. When you reinvest your dividends, interest, or capital gains, you're essentially putting your money back to work, allowing it to generate further returns.

This approach takes advantage of the transformative power of compound interest, where your earnings accumulate exponentially over time. By consistently reinvesting your profits, you're not just saving or earning – you're ***multiplying*** your wealth in a cycle of continuous growth. This reinvestment is the cornerstone of long-term wealth accumulation and a fundamental tactic for those aspiring to master the game of wealth.

Patience and Consistency

In the intricate dance of "The Wealth Game," patience and consistency are your allies. This is not a sprint to immediate riches; it's a marathon that unfolds over time. Patience allows you to weather the market's inevitable ups and downs, understanding that true wealth is built steadily. You must be emotionally stable, recognizing that every market is affected by cycles and your portfolio will feel them too. You make decisions based on your tolerance and the advice of an advisor and you stick to that advice. That is called consistency. Consistency in your investment approach ensures that you remain focused on your long-term goals, undeterred by short-term market fluctuations. Together, patience and consistency empower you to create your path toward sustainable financial growth.

Staying Informed and Educated

In the ever-changing economic landscape, staying informed and continually educating yourself are not just beneficial; they're essential. The environment of finance and investment is constantly changing, with new trends, regulations, and opportunities arising constantly. Staying informed of these changes is extremely important to making informed decisions that are connected to your financial goals. Engaging in continuous learning through books, financial news, seminars, and consultations with experts will develop your understanding and improve your strategic approach. It empowers you to navigate the complexities of the financial world with confidence , ensuring that your decisions are strategic, calculated, and informed.

Handling Investment Risks and Taxes

Being smart about the risks you take with your investments and understanding how taxes work is really important. Every time you invest money, there's a chance things might not go as planned. To deal with this, you should diversify your investments across different types (like stocks, bonds, or real estate), so if one doesn't do well, the others may do better. Diversification is a tool to hedge - or prepare against - investment risks, allowing an investor to find growth even in rough or difficult market conditions.

At the same time, it's important to know about taxes as it relates to your investments. When you make money from your investments, like selling them for more than you paid or getting dividends, you often have to pay taxes. Knowing this can help you make better choices, like picking investments that are tax efficient. This means that you will minimize your tax liability while increasing your profitability. By understanding both the risks and the tax implications, you can make your investment money work better for you.

You the Investor

Embracing your role as an investor is a significant milestone in The Wealth Game. It marks a transition from simply managing your wealth to actively growing it. Investing allows you to take control of your financial future, leveraging your savings and credit proficiency to build wealth. This chapter marks more than just the accumulation of knowledge; it signifies a call to action. It's an invitation to step into a role that extends beyond saving and managing credit, into the realm of actively growing and multiplying your wealth.

Investing, whether active or passive, is a crucial step in your financial journey. It's about making your money work for you, harnessing the power of the market to grow your assets. This is where you shift from being a participant in the game to being a strategist, plotting moves that compound over time to build substantial wealth. Once you step into this level, learning to invest is as simple as doing it. But the ideas that are on this level go far beyond the scope of this book. Whether you choose to engage actively in your investments or prefer a more passive approach, the goal remains the same: to achieve financial growth and stability.

1. **Active Investing:** This approach involves hands-on management of your investments. It's suitable for those who have the time, interest, and knowledge to closely monitor and make decisions about their investment portfolio.
2. **Passive Investing:** For those who prefer a less hands-on approach, passive investing might be more appropriate. This strategy typically involves investing in funds that track market indexes, requiring less time and expertise but still offering the benefits of market participation.

The Importance of a Support System

You don't have to go it alone. In fact, don't. Most of you have businesses or jobs that are far removed from the world of finance. Some of you are gifted in areas that are so far from finance that attempting to learn the nuance of investing would exhaust and frustrate you. To you, I say, "Build a team." Building a team of trusted advisors is key to navigating the complexities of the investment world successfully.

1. **Tax Advisors:** Understanding the tax implications of your investments is vital. A tax advisor can help you strategize to

minimize your tax liabilities and maximize your returns.

2. **Financial Planners:** A financial planner can help you align your investment strategies with your overall financial goals, ensuring a cohesive approach to wealth building.

3. **Other Financial Professionals:** Depending on your investment choices, you might also benefit from the expertise of other financial professionals, such as bankers, estate planners or investment brokers.

The Journey Ahead

As we prepare to summarize the contents of this book in the final chapter, let me congratulate you on how far you've come! Many may have picked up this book, but few will finish it. Even fewer will put into practice the content found in these pages. From establishing a wealth-building mindset to mastering budgeting and credit, and now stepping into the world of investing – each chapter has been a stepping stone to this point. I am excited for what comes next!

As you turn the pages to the final chapter, think of it not as the end, but as the beginning of your next move in The Wealth Game. The strategies, insights, and lessons shared in this book are tools to empower you, but the game's outcome depends on how you use them. Embrace your role as an investor with determination and foresight. Seek the counsel of experts, continuously educate yourself, and stay committed to your financial goals. The world of investing is rich with opportunities, and with the right approach, it can significantly elevate your position. Remember, you are the key player, and your moves determine your success!

Chapter Eight:
Final Thoughts

This book has been a comprehensive guide, a playbook of sorts, aimed at equipping you with the knowledge and strategies to navigate the complex world of personal finance and wealth building. Let's take a moment to revisit the key lessons from each chapter, consolidating our learning and preparing ourselves what comes next.

Chapter 1: The Time is Now

We began our game by understanding the urgency of starting our wealth-building journey. This chapter underscored the importance of seizing the moment to transform financial mindsets and habits. We looked at the wealth gap in black and brown communities, emphasizing the need for financial literacy and empowerment. The call was clear – the time to act, to change our financial trajectory, is now.

Chapter 2: Victory Requires Vision

Here, we delved into the value of having a clear vision for our lives, both socially and financially. A vision acts as a guiding star, keeping us focused and motivated, especially in challenging times. We explored how to craft a personal vision and the steps necessary to bring it to fruition, highlighting that success in The Wealth Game is as much about personal fulfillment as it is about financial achievement.

Chapter 3: The Power of Your Machine

This chapter was about shifting from an employee mindset to a business owner mindset. We emphasized seeing ourselves as a 'machine' – a business or career that can be developed and grown. The focus was on increasing personal value through skill acquisition, mentorship, and strategic career planning. We learned that by enhancing our 'machine,' we're better equipped to navigate the financial aspects of our lives.

Chapter 4: Master Money Management

Mastering money management is the cornerstone of financial stability. This chapter guided us through the essentials of effective budgeting and cash flow management. We learned the importance of a budget as a tool for financial control and the foundation for wealth accumulation. Mastering budgeting is not a one-time task but a continuous process.

Chapter 5: Be a Super Saver

Building on the principles of money management, we explored the art of saving. This chapter highlighted the importance of developing a savings mindset, focusing on delayed gratification and treating saving as a non-negotiable part of our financial plan. We discussed strategies for building an emergency fund, setting short-term and long-term saving goals, and the psychological aspects of spending and saving.

Chapter 6: Crush Your Credit

Here, the focus shifted to understanding and managing credit effectively. We discussed the importance of building a strong credit score and the benefits it brings, including access to financial opportunities and better loan terms. This chapter also provided insights into rebuilding credit and the pivotal role played by the major credit bureaus – Equifax, Experian, and TransUnion.

Chapter 7: Unleash the Investor

Advancing to the highest level of wealth building, this chapter was about embracing the role of an investor. We explored various investment options and the importance of building a diversified portfolio aligned with our risk tolerance and financial goals. The chapter emphasized the need for patience and consistency in investing and the role of advisors in guiding our investment strategies.

It's Go Time!

As we sum up the insights and strategies discussed in this book, it's important to remember that "The Wealth Game" is meant to educate and inform. While this book provides a comprehensive overview of personal finance and wealth-building strategies, ___it should not replace the personalized advice from a qualified financial professional.___ Each individual's financial situation is unique, and as such, professional guidance tailored to your specific circumstances is invaluable.

This journey is not just about enriching ourselves; it's about breaking the cycle of financial illiteracy in our communities. It's about launching our families into lives of purpose, stability, and prosperity.

Embrace the role of a wealth builder in your community. Share the knowledge and insights you've gained, and become a beacon of financial empowerment for those around you. Remember, every step you take in mastering this game not only elevates your financial standing but also contributes to the economic growth of your community.

In The Wealth Game, the ultimate victory is not measured in dollars and cents alone, but in the impact and legacy we leave behind. It's about creating a world where financial literacy and empowerment are not privileges but norms. So, let's continue to play this game with strategic wisdom, compassion, and a vision for a brighter, more financially secure future for all. This is just the beginning. The board is set, the pieces are in motion, and the path to victory is yours to chart. Play wisely, play boldly, and let's transform our financial destinies together!

www.ingramcontent.com/pod-product-compliance
Lightning Source LLC
Chambersburg PA
CBHW070047260726
48658CB00002B/779